stoned words & electric flowers

Jerry Palmer

volume 2

ISBN 979-8-3484-6783-8
First Printing 2023

Written from 1972-2023
Designed and printed in Rankin County, Mississippi
Cover uses Cooper Black and Cooper Nouveau typefaces
Body uses Minion Pro and the Cooper Nouveau typefaces

All images appearing in this book are courtesy of the Palmer Family Archives.

Paint Bucket Brigade Publishing
Rankin County, Mississippi

jerrypalmerauthor.com

Memory or Imagination

Still, I search for a love to fill the lonely feeling.
But the leaves change color as
around the corner she walks.
Once again will I be her fool.
Lady at first then came the truth.
All I gave was passion and my youth.
Maybe in another sky, will these memories leave,
I can try or when I die.
Her eyes are like the silent spring snow.
Forever is the stare but only the breeze is left.
To blow the ashes of time,
toward these green eyes and short hair.
As the birds left, they sang her name,
and now fly freely in the air, as I speak the same.

STOP
COMANCHE
PEAK
STOP
COMANCHE
PEAK

Dirty Windows

As I look though the painted window,
I see a world unsure, with it hard to write
my thoughts.
Sudden and unsure yet needing to be on the page.
But fate seems certain to guide us down the path.
To give in and become a carrier of burdens,
is hard to do when most thoughts are of you.
My actions seem of no importance.
Is it just what is left in the end that matters?
Can't let things be as they were
for so much has been undone.
Can it be grown back, or have we blossomed
too soon?

Flowers of Songs

If not for the sound of the guitars,
all would have been unbearable.
For it is true that time is the lock on all dreams.
Your thoughts have come to me by music.
Music is the key that unlocks the doors,
to paths of thoughts, in my world.
Songs have pasted by without my listening.
She also left long before I wanted her to,
if she had stayed the mist that haunts my soul,
would now be clouds giving rain to this parched soul.
I turned and the world stopped.
I saw her standing with her hair blowing in
the winds of time.
The chill made her cheeks red and her eyes shine,
Only for a moment did she smile and without
a word.
Said to dream not for today but for the time,
When I am but a flower in your mind or song,
Just wanting to sing along.

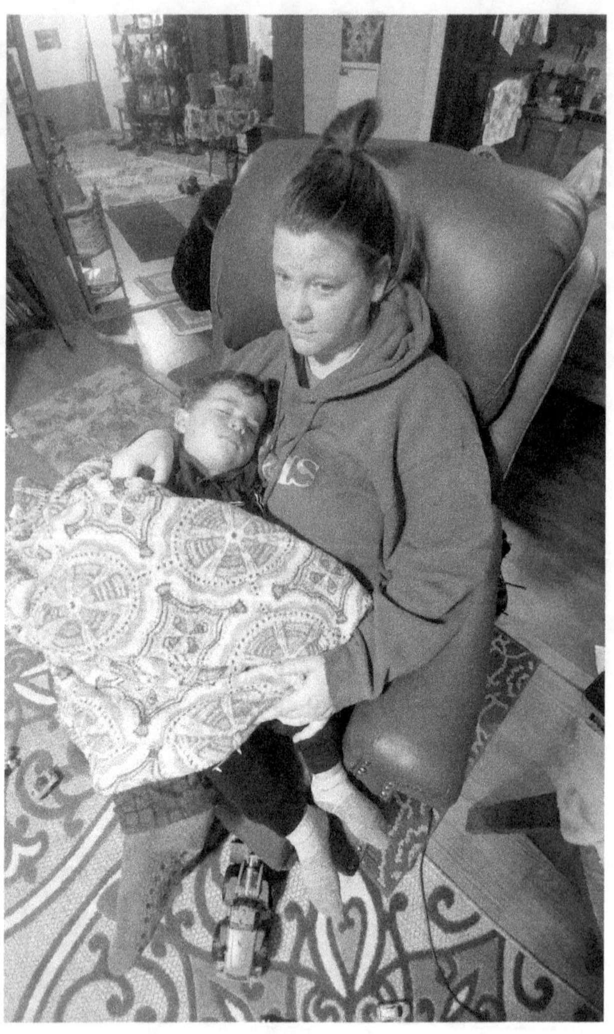

Sad-Eyed Lady

This is the flower of mind that must be cared for,
Without this, the candle of shadows dawn upon our
search for self.
The winds of forever blow the balloons of thought,
higher into the webs spun by the spiders of silver.
Which sparkles whenever the theme of smoke
dancing occurs.
Like a lively lady in the rays of color playing in
my dreams.
Only to puzzle her since she shoveled snow of white.
For you are here just as the glow appears,
when the flame flickers and ask the question.
Sad-Eyed Lady must I wait longer for my fate?

Robin Taylor

The day you came to town a glow of light shown
in the darkness.
A smile with the warmth of a sunny
southern morning.
Auburn the color of your hair,
the diamonds around you were not of your beauty.
With the rings and jewelry, you were the crown.
Now but a poem in my mind's papers.
A band played in your head, so my words are written
in a minute of sorrow as time must turn forward.
Wandering in a space large and yet often so small.
The light of your smile is on with my darkness
dimmed forever.
Because of the Robin which flew in the spring,
when the flowers were only beginning to unfold.

Ansel Adams
Buttons, Bolt Cutters & Barricades

Was Asked to Write

Why do you ask me to write?
Are you eager to read…are you in a hurry to learn?
To a box I send my words for they spill
from the page.
Treasures is all ya see, tuck them away.
With no one to share, place them in a chest then
forget the rest.
Space is all ya see, words run together like sand in
the sea.
The candle burns in the seashell soon to be gone.
Two men of stone guard the sign of hope.
A message is spread by the hanging waters,
alone a brass image shines for the world.
The mountains rise along the river, across which we
look for a bridge.
A stoned door unlocked to the world, so as my words
will be.
Still, you asked me to write, only if you will read.
Hear the wind, see all you can.
If you do not understand, start over and read it again.

April 20, 1974

Chain of Mind

The chain around my neck carries no cross.
Only a locket of thought is all it means.
Sliver in color… golden in dreams.
Wear it and you will see,
it is more than a chain to me…
Now and always, near and far…
See you reaching but you can't feel the stars…
Shine in the heavens, amaze here on Earth.
Are you real, if so when was your birth?
Tossed into this world having to prove your worth
Is it better now than it was at first?
When the days were long
and the nights flew by.
Chain of mind is but a trinket you wear
like a ribbon or barrette in your hair.

Stoned Girl

Stream of diamonds gave forth these gems.
Came in the rough and uncut,
but still a sparkle she gave.
Therefore, this gem I tried to save.
To my surprise there wasn't a gem inside, Only a stone of coal,
dark without a soul.
With a message that read, I know your heart and how it bled.
This is one treasure you can't own, for if you did
It would be wasted as it went to your head.

Ladies in Satin

Cry tears of red lace, their love goes easy.
So, with their minds, take it slower for you know
there's still time.
Time to rest… so to look your best.
Time to delay for you know he's on the way.
Time is for now but somehow for tomorrow it waits.
Cause it needs someone like you to take its place.
Always in a hurry to get things done
most don't even matter, yet onward you go.
If not for yourself surely for the show.
To be arm candy and able to
silence a room with just a glance
and the hope of what will come soon.

Last Heartache

True that in time this girl I did find.
Now in time she wants to leave me behind…
Not much to do… tell her this thought,
and leave it to you.
Cause I doubt if she will listen
onward with the tears,
continue to crawl through the years.
Gone never to return… at least
not in the same way you went away.
Time helps the pain and turns tears to rain.
Walking down this path knowing it won't last,
makes remembering a treasure
and forgetting a task.
Not for the weak, not for the easy.
All for the heartaches of the future
and of the past.
Hoping this will be the last.

Too Dry for Roses

Voice of the future talking to the past.
Tell you nothing will last, except the cement
and glass.
It might stay of fear.
It might leave in fright,
but your memory is clear, and it shall always be near.
Too dry for roses, too wet for cactus.
When the world is barren… may there be for us,
two wildwood flowers and a bag of seeds.
Perhaps a little more for our needs.
Jupiter could be a sun, I could learn not to run.
Yet whatever it decides to do, here I'll sing
with a cement heart,
With a rose-colored glass from which to start.

Wagon Tracks at Brushy Creek

Wink in a time…
Time in a wink…
If all the roses were red,
enough would have been said.
Repeating myself mattered more than once.
My trouble is I can't tell the ending from the front.
Sad but it's true and I'm talking to you.
This and that, kiss and spat.
Still are we searching for where it's at?
Could I be the moon…
Could she be the womb…
Win or lose, coward or friend…
Tell me please is it the beginning or the end?

Lisa

Light in your smile, brings me cheer, brings me joy.
Piece of crystal, you said was your heart.
Handle With Care…
Sharp around the edges, touch only if you dare.
May I ask you dear, will someone be near?
If not nearby, then how far away?
For the further you fall the closer you are…
To the opening or to the door.
Cause before you fell you wanted a rose.
New Dawn is what you got, so the story goes.
Long before it was a thing in your heart,
It was a piece of crystal hanging on a string.
Not knowing the love to this world you would bring.

Nelson

Don't and do, will but wouldn't.
Can and can't…
Lost in rhyme… I saw you this time.
Hiding beneath a jar… thrown into the ocean,
kite in the wind… raising then falling
I miss you my friend… you searched the desert,
While I searched the fields… we found them both
Sonoran Desert toad and Psilocybin cubensis.
Played along the way… touching the future
from the past, your books contain magic
while mine tell of an adventure,
Noah Nukes / Al Most
and how you always treasured being the host.
From solar panels to metal skulls, smoke bombs
and bottles of mead…always in laughter.
Offering help for those in need.

…Ken Nelson aka Albert Most / Noah Nukes
A true friend indeed

ERA
YES
BARNWELL
PROUD
ELIZABETH PEACE
Shawn

Smoke & Shrooms

Minutes of red, spots of blue.
Lady by the wall never want to use you.
First your eyes were red then they faded to blue.
Now you're looking, now you're not.
Going to Austin, searching for pot...
gonna turn the time, or at least make it rhyme.
Now in grace, now in haste looking for something.
I once saw in space... touched it for a moment.
Held me forever...was this dumb or sort of clever?
If not for you then for one of them.
You came with me but left with him...

Mavis Belisle... Smiles

What can I say — known you for only a day.
Lost sight for years yet you returned the smiles…
An S on each end and a mile in the middle.
The longest word in the world.
Battles you have fought — never raised a hand in anger
Signed all the papers — never concerned with
the danger.
You were the light- helping me find the way,
To learn how to make change — like the sunshine
helps make hay…Thank You

NUCLEAR
WAR
IS BAD FOR
CHILDREN

Talking in Your Sleep

Slow does it seem, short is the dream.
But once I awoke it was you who spoke.
You spoke of a tiny dancer and a queen of hearts.
Asking me where does it end, where does it start?
Robbed of a treasure that never was mine.
Did I sleep too long, or did I wake too soon?
If I die before I sleep give this to K. Susan
and all my writings can she keep.
If I live as I do — may we look forward
and I somehow be near you.
So hot this summer that the sun ruins the day,
Not much to do but a little to say.
To somehow to be remembered, is important to me.
For if not at least there was a shot…
these words are what you got.

June 1977

DANGER
ALLIGATORS
WATER MOCCASINS

Overturned Stones

Glazed but never polished gem in the rough.
Polisher I am and here will I be found.
Searching in the mud and on drier ground.
For hidden jewels or perhaps a complete crown.
Overturned all the stones looked under each one,
hoping to find something shiny or a rock
to lean upon.
All is deeper than I can dig.
Perhaps I need a shovel instead of a spoon.
Perhaps I could search in the sun instead
of under the moon.

Signed My Tears

I heard a song — you helped me right along.
Always come back to you — kind of strange
but it sure is true.
Ponytails I planted, ribbons I saved.
All I would give if a mere moment would become
clear in the haze.
Could be in vain then again could be worth the pain.
What to lose, what to gain?
If not tomorrow perhaps today.
Ask you to stay only to watch you walk away.
Decided to slow down even came back to
a small town.
Never been surprised more than those days looking,
for someone like you yet she was not to be around
Only felt the shock of you leaving never again
to be found.

NO NUKES

COMANCHE PEAK REPORT — TIME IS RUNNING OUT...

The Comanche Peak nuclear power plant, located only 40 miles from Dallas-Fort Worth, is scheduled to begin operating soon. Over 100 tons of uranium fuel is due to be delivered to Reactor 1 this spring from the east coast. The fuel will be shipped regardless of whether the plant has been licensed to operate and with serious questions about safety still being investigated.

This is a request for your support in building a nonviolent blockade and citizens' reprieve to protest Texas' first nuclear power plant.

If Comanche Peak operates:

* We can expect to see significantly more cancers and birth defects throughout North Texas, including the D-FW area, from planned and accidental releases of low and high level radiation.

* Highly radioactive waste will be stored at Comanche Peak and then possibly shipped for reprocessing into nuclear bombs.

* Electric utility rates will skyrocket as the burden for operating the $5 billion plant falls heaviest on residential consumers.

* The area from the Oklahoma border to below Waco will be threatened with a catastrophic accident that the government estimates would cause 6,000 deaths, 14,000 injuries and $117 billion in property damage, making the land uninhabitable for centuries.

Comanche Peak nuke,

If you've been sitting on the fence, get down and get active.

If you've been involved with anti-nuke work before, we need you now more than ever.

Work for a nuclear-free future in your own backyard.

Can a few concerned citizens armed only with audacity and purpose bring to a halt the combined folly of government, industry, power and wealth? The only answer we know is the most comforting and terrifying of answers:

ANYTHING IS POSSIBLE

COMANCHE PEAK NONVIOLENT BLOCKADE

Lost Notes

Often, I write in fright — often when in a tight.
Sometimes to ease the pain.
Even write while hearing the rain.
Not very easy might be a little teasy.
Lost a tear once while I cried.
Swore I would write still I died.
Might quit after looking inside,
finding the heat so hot it could fry.
Flew around the air — never even moved the chair.
Often thought of peace and that we all need
some relief.
Just couldn't grasp ahold —
now I'm wandering looking for my soul.
Lost and found, circle go round.
Crossed a river never learned to swim.
Passed underneath, lost the sky
cause I got mud in my eye.
Star lite, star bright let me fly again tonight.
Wayward flight takes all my might.

D. Delaney

She gave me something I can forever save.
Then when I'm asked what Delaney gave…
I really don't know for I never let it show.
Think of you and it makes me feel good.
And in your time perhaps you will write
some rhyme.
Keep all your goodness and live for all time,
Or for a little while at least.
I was there and had a feast.
Leg of lamb, sandwich of ham.
No better dish could be found.
These days were soft, these days were few.
These days were of you, these days I'm lonely too.
After you're gone maybe there will be another
To carry my song but if not, this will do.
For empty it will seem without you.

Summer Run
July 1977

Questions Needing Answers

Shall I write without a pen?
Can a word start and not end?
Sad but true — I never met a person as strange as you.
No one to answer, no one to tell.
Living without this is equal to a stream
without bream.
Pieces of crystal floating through time.
Can you smoke quietly, or do I blow you smoke rings
from here?
Can you hold them in your hands or wear them
as a headband?
Ten together can match the world, nine can trip
and fall.
If you aren't the one, then who is first?
As these words have no meaning at all.

Slow Burn

If it be yours to run and burn
then take this torch and set the fields on fire.
Justice to the one who reaches and does not tire.
Stuck to a page as if the light shined brighter,
when I push and find what had been written
was only mine to claim.
Colors grow brighter then they begin to fade.
No colors to wear only white does she keep.
Only for the pure and not the weak shall the wine
be poured.
Only for the worthy shall the fruit be stored.
Woe to you, who run without foes.
Push no harder for this is as far as it goes.

Once Then Again

Life be no island and I be no shell,
to walk with you and hear the stories you could tell.
Enchantment heard now only by the wind.
Sitting on a pier, grateful you are this near.
Tell me once more so it will become clear.
Love me once, love you again — all we have
is time to spend.
Hard to come by, impossible to keep
the moments we have and the love we seek.
Upon the corners of the day my mind
slips and thoughts of you carry me away.
Never will it be but always worth the chance
to catch a glimpse of your smile…
To feel the passion on your lips.

River Flow

Dumped my feelings into the river as they
floated away
all I could do is shiver.
No use are they to me might as will lose them
to the sea.
Since my heart and my soul seem to have left me
without hope.
Don't feel bad — it's not the first love gone sour,
But my — I must say — ours didn't last but an hour.
Yet a hour of the best, a hour to test,
what was given or what must be taken.
The river needs to flow cleaning the land,
making another bend, enriching the soil,
carrying away all our madness
while turning rocks into clay.

Snails... Cahaba River

Looking For Space… Nothing to Save
Not enough space to walk,
not enough space to run,
not enough to give your all,
only enough to crawl.
You used to hunt for shells,
Now you hurt for fame,
Should have saved the pictures,
Then you'd have had something to share.
The shells are broken, turned into sand.
You stand barefooted, reaching tho nothing is there.

Mae

If love can be seen — it was in your walk — upon
the screen.
Five may double to make ten and what will
it become when the movies ends?
Do you have the same walk?
Perhaps even the same talk?
From your words it seems to me that you wish
to be free.
If it's not too much to ask, walk slower —
for watching you is such a task.
If there was ever a blonde whom in this world,
I was very fond; it would be you.
Since you outshine the sun.
Gotta be you, who proved blondes have more fun.

Dollar Date

Sitting in the curve, while living by the curb.
Passing the time, thinking it would be nice if you
had a few dimes.
Jack's Tamales ten cents each, free crackers and a
coke for a dime.
Take her to dine — wondering if you can make it —
and if she'll have the time?
Go to the park to try and fly the kite.
If things go right — you'll get off the ground tonight.
In five years' time — may I find you.
May you remember me,
may we both be doing fine.

Flower of Time

Stream of beauty flowing thru this life,
with the freshness of youth, searching for a truth.
Grace and wonder have touched your soul,
all who know you, this they behold.
Your being here is enough to declare,
it's not the moon that moves the tides,
it's your breathing that stirs the air.
Causing comets to freeze giving,
a warm feeling to the summer breeze.
The length of your hair, the song in your voice
give reason to pause hoping to
make the right choice.
Marking of time is like watching
a flower grow, slow and easy.
Never meant to last.
All pointing to the future
while remembering the past.
Flowers to grow, words to find
thanks for it all and the
moments of your time.

Solidarność
SOLIDARITY

Solidarność

Olga

You're so young — to do — as you have done.
So smooth — always catching the bar,
never missing a move.
At home in the air — and your happiness the world
can share.
Yet to speak the wrong words — perhaps never again
to be heard.
If your medals begin to get heavy — drop them
by your side.
Rest awhile — for you have a way to go.
Little girl from Russia has such greatness —
It only begins to show.

Pretty Words

Now She walks alone, the world is hers to roam.
Gave back the ring, with it all the sounds
that love brings.
Don't take it hard, try to remember what
you left it for.
Care not for keeping the pace, all this doesn't matter,
it's really not a race. Glass hearts and a ring…
Pretty words are often used, pretty words can
also bruise.
Gave it all away — the day you gave back the ring,
with it all — the sounds love brings.

Little Flower

With the beauty of sunrise,
You grow in the meadows of a mountain range
covered by snow.
Is your blooming to be seen by our eyes,
or is it deep within that your true glamour lies?
If picked and placed in a vase, would you begin
to wilt
and all your features go to waste?
May I plant you in my garden?
To watch and care until the days end.
Or it be your wish — I'll leave you in the meadow
so, your fragrance will grace the world again.

To Jan Black
English 201
Hinds Jr. College 1972

Bloom Where You're Planted

While seeing the world as a flower,
We drank wine and danced for hours.
Will it bloom again or be gone after a quick shower?
Rain from the clouds… water from the sky…
Cool this passion now that our heads are turned.
Much has been seen, much has been learned.
Wouldn't be a bit surprised… if what I see isn't real,
Tho heaven awaits just behind your eyes.
Saw you with a friend, flower in hand.
Will she leave you wanting more than petals and
a stem?
Long was your hair… ice was your stare.
Sore was my soul as we met at the fair.
Long am I laughing, long will I care.

WOODLAND
SWAMP LOOP
MEADOW LOOP
Rules & Regulations
This area belongs to the City of Grenada
and is a wildlife sanctuary.
It is free and open to the public.
Leave No Trace!
Carry out ALL trash, pick up after your pet,
do not drive on wet roads.
Allowed:
hiking, fishing, dogs, camping, kayaking
Not Allowed:
dumping, littering, shooting firearms,
hunting, trapping, fireworks, driving
motorized vehicles off road, removing
plants or animals
This area is within the City Limits of Grenada.
It is patrolled by the Grenada Police Department.
Violators are subject to fines or arrest.

Park Walk... Small Talk

Words for tomorrow I dare not say...
But for tonite I want you to stay.
Last time I saw you... was loved and left.
Now you touch my soul and sent me away.
Spread your laughter... join me in play.
Hold me close make the winter seem like May.
Sit by the fire, dream of you... just to get higher.
Walking among the clouds as they kiss the ground.
Singing this song... trying to get along.
As the moments of memory and imagination
are as clay, always I ask will you
love me and leave me only to return
another day?
Not enough of you to go around,
spread so thin being an anchor
for your crew as your soul
wants to dance in the wind.
Leaving you not knowing what to do...

Pirate

Wanted to see all your shores.
Now that it's over — wondering looking back over
my shoulder.
Wasn't much that was missed, caught the breeze.
Sailed away with ease.
Once met a Lady, cute and spicy,
nice with a touch of naughty.
Sent me her picture, for this I was richer.
Asked her to stay while I went away.
Upon my return this I did learn.
She went away with a pirate.
Leaving me a note…twenty years ago She wrote…
This doesn't matter for together we'll never be.
But still, I'll always wonder, what did the Sea give you
That couldn't have been found for free?

For Tomorrow

At this point I will start — onward thru the fog.
I saw a robin thought he was the last bird.
Cried out for his life — yet there was — so much noise,
keeping me from being heard.
Looked at the moon — as if she had something to say.
Then I passed only to become a speckle of clay.
For tomorrow I have dug a well.
Only to fill it with bulbs in trying
to climb back to the top.
Starting at the bottom and building
no sides leave only the top to show
knowing there is still more to go.
Dug thousands of bulbs and still
have a few more to find.
Most hiding in plain sight or
wrapped in some vines.
Always carry a shovel and
keep an eye out for trouble.

Puzzle

Playing this game isn't very difficult,
yet there are times it becomes absurd.
Looking for the pieces to put them in place.
Some are of wood; some are of lace.
Some are lost here on Earth — some are lost in Space.
Careful to pick the one that fits and not her sister.
Looking too fast can cause a blister.
Looking too slow caused us to miss her.
Working along the edges with nothing in the middle,
Gives a sense of hope when there is so little.
Bumped the table then lost my way.
Still looking for those pieces that blew away.
Or the ones which came with the Flood
and are here to stay.

Hanging Moss Creek
Flood of 2020

Fence Rows

For the rose that didn't grow,
for all the things I'll never know.
Was given a green thumb or does this count?
For now, vines are entwined in the treetops.
The honeybees are not from here,
Tho the honey is sweet — more birds are needed.
Dead branches have a use — cut into mulch
and a place for to hang moss.
Morning Glory grows on the fence row,
Seeds spread wherever the winds blow.
Katrina Rose please grow for this gardener
loves the Lady so...

U.S. GEOLOGICAL SURVEY
$250 DOLLARS FINE FOR DISTURBING THIS MARK
REFERENCE MARK
NO 1
SIGNAL
1931

Day to Stay

Turn the day as if it were a page.
Think of lines to write as if I were in a rage.
Only to see later it's just another stage, just
another play.
Turning again into another day.
The sunrises since you're not there.
Haven't a thought, haven't a care.
Bless the morning air, bless the way I look at
early day.
Wishing in a way the dawn could stay.
Fought the nite — along with the shadows,
the figures in the dark.
Realizing morning is just the start.
The world's coming down fast but it's still miles away.
She won't see me, so I turn away.
Up I ran, up I ran; feeling as if one reaches.
Yet seeing no hand, like swimming in a sea that has
no land.
No place to catch my breath, no place to make
a stand.
So up I ran — up I ran.

Emerald Green

Sat in a room — full of music but couldn't hear
the tune.
Listened for notes, seeing only a broom.
Sweeping away the waves, keeping away the gloom.
Thought of something beautiful, so I write
this to you.
Looked into your eyes; emerald green they seem.
Again, something beautiful with daydreams of you.
Yet dear girl, I want something, and I think it's you.
Give me a favor for whatever you do,
don't change them to blue.

Dragon Glass

If there were dragons — who flew in the sky.
I would be digging bulbs… barely getting by.
If there will be maidens… always to cry.
Come all knights in rusty armor… to save the Lady.
By dropping names… To stop all
that could harm her…
Giving her all the flowers that grow…
Wanting to help plant them
but it's not to be.
Dig bulbs, replant for flowers
only others will see.
Dragons of briars… vines of venom
look but don't touch, for it
was she who sent them.
Carrying the potions and remedies
for all that ail you… all that can cure.
More not to ask for, no more to give.
Dragonflies and floating seeds
can make more of this
if there is need.

Roses

In fields of roses — you can find a thorn.
In the days you see — none like the one when you were born.
In picking the roses you pause by a stream
to rest your soul and quench the thirst.
There She was waiting, always to be first.
Asked Her name — She said not word.
Just a look of silence and a wave of Her hand.
Told more than any man can understand.
How could such beauty,
How could such pain
be upon the same plant
and Rose be her name?
Some are nearly thornless others wear razors
not from the meek does she seek favors.
Almost bare-rooted while cloaked in petals
this be a flower worth precious metals.
Those with fragrance cause calming
and the lure of a trance.
Those without scent… are like
a pretty girl, who doesn't like
to dance.

Empty Pages

Back to the roses — back to the thorns.
Things like this happen — you were well warned.
You found an old book with its pages well worn.
Told of a knight and a maiden near a field of thorns.
In taking a chance, from the book this page I did tear.
From the book of time, I have torn a page.
Destined to wander looking afar,
to chance upon the maiden with book
missed its cover and the last page.
Always to be picking roses, thinking of dragons
that fly.
How could it be time has passed me by?

June 13, 1975

Star and What You Are

Rings and bracelets, buckles and beads.
All that sparkles you wear as a crown.
Given by one whom you view as a clown.
Arm candy and a trophy wife,
these are your victories, earned in this life.
As you continue, I make you a toast.
Till this day is remembered,
may life grant you the most.
Read this again not having any doubts,
For whom it is to and about.

HOLE TO
ANOTHER UNIVERSE

COLLEGE OF CONSTRUCTIVE HELL RAISING
Parva Cumulaverunt
"Think Like an Organizer"

Burning the Stars

Stars burn forever then they burnout.
Black holes are the empty space
created after the burn.
Comets are tears of a nova present and past,
weeping at this moment, knowing it is the last.
When two comets met, one place becomes another.
Future is the present we longed for in the past.
Now with the ice beginning to melt,
with the giant trees starting to leave,
does the warmth of our sun
really begin to burn?
Always talk in the shade, lay
in the cool grass.
Hiding from the future… longing for the
past you never knew, lost are
the stories and the sky which was blue.
Here must we start to slow the
fire burning with our greed…
Don't keep taking more than you need.

Standing in Heavy Water

Sorry to my soul — as the pages begin to unfold.
All the things I heard but wasn't really told.
No more is the mighty dollar equal to the gold.
Are the falls we take to be in vain?
Do the shots we're given scar the veins?
Tell me now or the question will always remain,
Are me thoughts always to be circles,
and do me brain wrinkle under the strain?
Sorry to my soul — in trying to drown the feeling
hiding in the ink.
Lost forever more poems to the darkness
than the late snow loses flakes.
Flakes of this stone slowly chipping away.
Too fast for nature, too slow man.
Too heavy for water so here I will stand.

2 8'99

High Water

On the platform waiting for time to pass
or the muddy waters to rise.
Rise to the top of the levee.
Full are the creeks, full are the streams.
Full is the old Pearl River — ugly thing.
Sure, gives us all a shiver.
To survive the Flood of '79,
Took a good motorboat, sandbags and a lot of time.
No more looking for what you had is gone.
If not washed down the Pearl, then surely the Strong.

ABSOLUTELY
NO NUKES!

Haze

Time passed by — never asked why.
Nor should it have to answer.
For we labeled it- letting it fly.
Here and now, I wonder aloud — will there be rain,
or just another smog cloud?
In the days of Summer 1979.
Knew it was hot — all cement and glass.
We need more trees — live oaks
not Bermuda grass.
Combing through the thatch,
wondering where the water goes,
after it leaves the faucet and
drains down the hose.
It flows quickly to the concrete
street, soon the Trinity River
it will meet.
One good rain and one good
flush and all this liquid is
in the Gulf.

Future Daze

Dreamed of these things only
to lose them in the morning.
Cast away from today in a matter
I would rather not say.
Of the habits we need to change
Of my friends that are strange
All in a moment these will appear to be distant
Yet forever remain so near.

Sept. 1979

Direct Action
Seabrook May 24
Occupation / Blockade
for more information call:
Coalition for Direct Action at Seabrook

Note

Decade has passed.
Amazing how long they last.
Not like a year — nor like a day.
A decade passed in its own true way.
All for one, one for all.
Seven have passed, just hoping that's not all.
Notes upon the page hoping for importance.
Seeing time in the seasons,
knowing why but not the reasons.
Notes in the decades I spent
away from you, paper pages and songs
I heard in concert halls and
from birds in the hills can never
say enough about the way I feel.

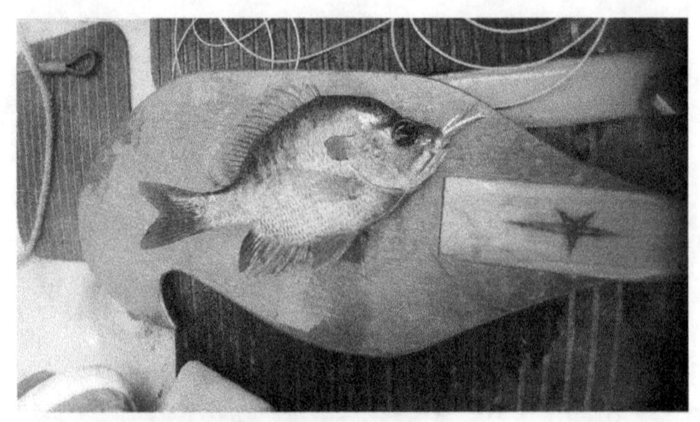

Blue Lines to Brown Waters

Back down the roads, around the corners
and pass the ditches.
Under the bridges lay the blue lines,
containing the fishes.
Brown water on a cloudy day makes for good casting,
if the limbs aren't in the way.
Small creeks, deep holes give me adventure.
If I can reach them with or without permission.
Only use poppers so much,
reaching under the surface to use droppers
That's where I find fly rod benders, colorful fishes
& most answers to my wishes.

Questions?

Seeking answers turn many ways,
If you need four perhaps you will find five.
Days of darkness, nites of lite.
Is there a forever?
Or is today to be stronger than tonite?
Smoke to rise, smoke to hide.
Smoke for answers that come from inside.
Perhaps the truth plays a hiding game.
Perhaps we are lost — all looking for the same.

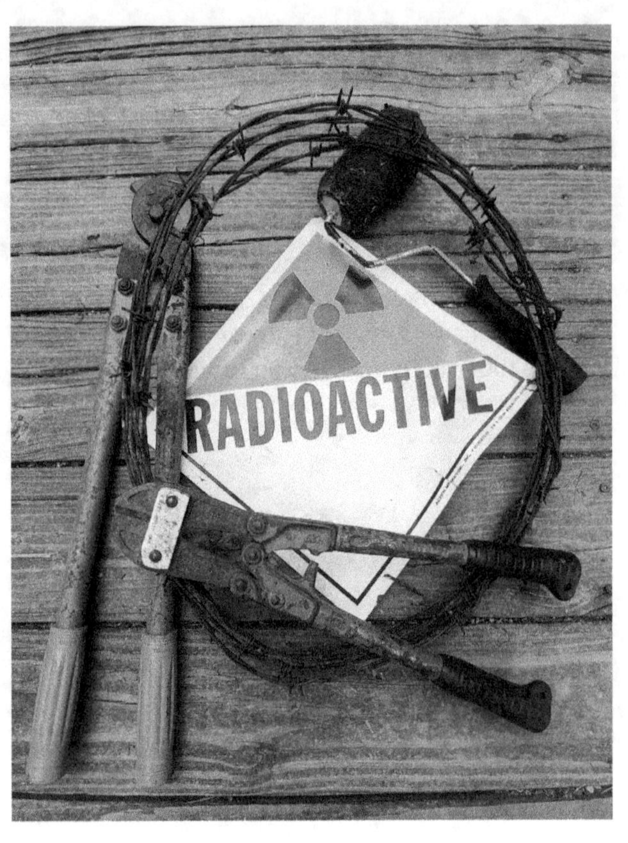
RADIOACTIVE

Rule Change...
House Rules

Once to know, always to care.
Is our country strong, can we right the wrong.
Hidden creek runs so smooth,
down the middle of a river.
Doesn't know the rules —
Surely not ones made by fools.
Yes, we can change — for we have the tools.
Corporations in self-regulation
kinda like being a warlord trying
not to fight — ain't gonna happen.
Profit is the mission — pollution is the cost.
Onward to the goal — progress without a soul.
All for the dollar — cast away
the beauty of the earth.
Never listened to her holler.
Yet in the end, we'll play by
her rules… Nature bats last.

Pollinators of the World
May 4-May 20, 2017
Upstairs Gallery
The Cole Art Center @ The Old Opera House

From There to Here

Few are the answers, many are the lies.
Between the lines is where the truth is found.
Caring for the planet is like hugging the ground.
Small be the holes we dig to bury our souls.
Huge is the mess we have left, digging for our goals.
Replace what has been taken,
With compost and charcoal, stir it slowly.
Watch as the growth unfolds.
Not to say this is original,
not to say that it is old.
Just to say it drifted in from my soul.

June 1979 & October 2022

Cactus and Fire Ants

Thinking about trying to continue or exit stage left.
Crawled thru the darkness — carried only my sword
or what's left on it.
Not wanting to bother, not wanting to wait.
Everything else was left on the shelf.
Sandcastles washed away — most are in ditch banks
Or in roadside dumps along the way.
Trees are short and seldom grow tall, some are just
shrubs not trees at all.
Pretty little bushes, dainty little plants —
All they're good for is to attract ants.
Cactus and mesquite have left quite a mark.
Fact is their statement is so strong
You can't even touch the bark.
Thorns a plenty, along with fire ants.
Too hot to touch, to sore to eat.
Best to hope for is to stay on your feet.
As a hawk flew above looking for love,
Or just for a quick lunch of a dove.

Make War No More

Of the chapters of war
this will be the
thirty thousandth at least...
It hasn't started yet,
but I'm sure you've heard.
In the sands of the Nile,
in the mountains of Persia,
in the streets of Russia
and in the roads of Portland.
Fighting over water, oil and mud.
Not to be looking down,
Just what I saw when I looked around.

Black Moon

Girl in the black veil walks the hills all alone.
Trying in vain to hear his song.
Crying won't help the things she did wrong.
Sold her man for sliver, spent the coins of her soul.
Lost it all to a drifter.
Hide she cannot for his words — haunt her being.
"Wear this veil — speak your words to the wind.
Run forever — tears you won't shed, not upon my bed.
Not even in hell, lost in your mind — this is where
you will always dwell"

December 16, 1974

Bleeding Heart

You wear your heart upon your sleeve.
You wonder why you so easily bleed.
You must care for this heart,
if not, it will tear you apart.
Your love is not but a seed.
Cast it to the wind — a life of wonder will you spend.
Plant it, let it grow.
Seed to soil contact is all you needed to know.
In your life — you may see rain — you may see snow.
Care greatly for this heart and years from now,
It will still glow.

December 21, 1974

Water Under the Bridge

With stones gathering moss
Blow wind, blow her near.
Shine moon — give her light to return soon.
Give her my message, before the snow melts.
For when the sun shines there will be someone else.
She'll be left behind or at best second in line.

December 25, 1974

The stones were overturned and
the moss washed away.
Tree fell into the stream
With the sand silting in the gravel bars
The river cannot run — we cannot hide.
We stand on the bridge tossing
rose petals at time as tears fill
the muddy stream and the dreams grow.
As moss appears again on the
stoned words of my mind.

Mark... aka Wacky

We started foolish so we have nothing to lose.
We can run any race — on any course we choose.
After we started it's not too bad.
It's close to the end when things are sad.
Yet from now till then — let us be glad.
For the time we shared and the laughs we had.
We never lost anything till we lost someone.
Cotton in spoons — smoke filled rooms.
Bending points to keep from being straight.
Look beyond the pain — try and stay sane.
Think you're going crazy or is it just being lazy.
Not sure but the room sure looks hazy.

Quote:
If I had known I was going to live this long…
I've took better care of myself.

…Mark Neely

Images

Being so close — one gets cold while the other roasts.
Giving the same gifts is not very good,
But you're doing as you felt you should.
You live in the same way — being one another.
Guess it's not hard to decide what to say.
Two is different while one is the same.
If I kissed, you — which would say her name?
One eyes are blue, one eyes are green.
Ones loves peaches, Her sister likes cream.
Not the same as twins, for they are just friends.
When time comes around again, there's
the beginning
or is it the end?
Where will you start, where will you end.
One a pot stirrer, the other is the glue.
Only really knew one, wishing could have
known two.

December 29, 1974 – November 2022

Dee... Mushroom Mystery

As I walked into the room, my eyes gave me away.
"Want some of that" ...was all she had to say.
Paint your face in words yet nothing I have said...
you heard.
Now are we wandering?
Yes, so it seems looking in the darkness... seeing
many shadows,
sharing many dreams.
Care for nothing and nothing will you lose.
This is how I felt, now and forever to write the blues.
Once you left what other way could I chose?
Paid in time for something lost... now looking
for pieces
or perhaps for some clues.
If you ask of, what lady do I write, can't ready say
For I was trippin that nite, my eyes gave me away.
Of course, I miss her but these things you see.
Don't just happen to me.
She said her name was "Dee" and was headed
to Florida
to explore the Gulf Sea & perhaps we could meet
another day.

Fire Towers

Do they still keep watch in the towers?
Or have the rangers left never to return?
Now the fires are close and the winds are strong.
Blowing in all directions no place to run, no place to hide.
Burning of the fields increases the yield.
Dragging chains and mufflers can make the sparks,
Just as cigarettes tossed into the grass.
This ain't your ashtray… what more to say?
Tossed out the windows forming wind rows
at the stop lights and mounds fire ants
didn't build, nicotine butts and filters
lasting two days past forever…
Bugs and bees come and go.
Fire towers are removed as oaks
fall and are replaced with pine.
Wonder about the cough and the cost
as the fires grow hotter…
and a good shade tree is harder to find.

OPEN

Hercules Beetle (Dynastes Tityus) at Lycoris Rose

Lightning Bugs out of the Jar…
Can ya tell me all the things you know?
If ya can, I'll show ya places no one else can go.
Things y'all never see in a show.
After we've returned the days will sparkle,
the nights will have a glow.
Learn to know lightning bugs and wildflowers
as kids,
Catch them in jars, tighten the lids.
Release them after a while is something
I hope we did.
Just so you know… all bugs don't bite.

COLONIAL COUNTRY CLUB
JACKSON COURSE
POSTED
PRIVATE PROPERTY

Last Place

Prizes I have had — ribbons I have worn.
A picture of your face is one I can't erase.
Fading moments and the time we spent,
is gone all but a trace.
Sad are these times for some —
sadder are the times we face.
Now we struggle to make more money,
or to get out from under rubble.
They talk of falling but they have already fell.
How can you tell someone softly,
if all they do is yell?
Crosses are worn, bullets have torn,
I weep with the world as she suffers our scorn.
Are the days really lost?
Will time bring you closer?
Will the prize be worth the cost?

Evening Star

Morning came with the light of the sun.
Dew upon the grass as a new day was born.
Just as I the morning is passing and cannot stay.
The making of dreams, takes so long it seems.
To wish what you want, just to get what you need.
Be rid of the old bush yet plant its living seed.
Took long enough to get here but we haven't
traveled far except for the excuses…
my goodness what a traveler you are.
Write your book… from the notes you took.
Can't wait to take a look.

NONVIOLEN
CT ACTION

Embers Remain

Shall the fire burn itself out?
With no more fuel to be had,
does this make you weary or make you sad.
Ashes and smoke as well as the flame,
claim many victims as you reach for the fame.
Heat and warmth we cannot do without.
Yet the fires rages and it won't go out.
Some plants need fire, all need rain.
Here we stand looking… never to be the same.
Comfort is king and I'll be a hypocrite
if this isn't said… Love the fan
blowing air as I rest my head.
Warmth from the furnace and the
light made at night… Mostly for
watching t.v. but occasionally reading
what others did write.
All this said... The poison power
has us by the grid.
Yet to save the lifestyle
changing the source is all we did.

Sparkle...

Girl with baton in hand, were you meant to
be here or in another land?
You dance like the ladies of a time past.
Catching each toss that nears your hand.
Have you lived in a valley that knows only spring?
For when you walk all the flowers shimmer,
the bees fly but don't sting,
When you talk it's as the wind stops,
and the parakeets begin to sing.
Walk with me now, bring your wand.
Cast a spell that we may sail on a swan.

WIDE
AWAKES.
1860.

James Marshall Hendrix

Gone to the dahlias — where the angels play.
Coved by a dust — cast by the heavens.
Going at early or late twenty-seven
Hoping to find one to trust.
Will I be there before the gate closes?
If so, perhaps I'll bring you some roses.
Learn your songs along the way.
Then we can ask Jimi why he went away.

August 11, 1974

Burning Letters from Woodstock

On a bench from I first saw you,
To the love in your eyes yesterday.
I carry something special which will never go away.
We drank to tomorrow never caring or feeling
sorrow.
You came from a friend and to a friend did you end.
Send me a card asking me to come see you marry.
No ride or way to be there.
Sat and burned your letters,
leaving tear drops on each one.
Cards mean nothing, so with the paper,
which ties you in marriage.
What you have belongs to you and the ages,
Not written upon paper pages.
Wind blows then who knows
where he will sail.
Lasting thru time is your protection from this gale.
May your nights be lit by fancy matches.
When you smoke don't forget
who shared with you that first toke.
Creating a ring of smoke, giving me eternal hope.
Burning pages written across the years,
mixing tears with rain — seeing your love,
has healed all the pain…

Small Candles Light the Way

Cast your flame to the wind… leaving no ashes.
Asking not how but always when.
Leave now while there's still room,
seek what you long for, just be easy with the spoon.
Lift the sparkles to the stars, live life while it's free.
Burn the candles in windows, placed in colored jars.
Touch softly and fingers will not burn.
No matter how hard we push back,
The world will always turn.

Behind Those Pretty Eyes

Look very closely and you will be surprised.
All the true things outweigh the lies.
Do we go on or do we part inside?
My thoughts are unless so your dream can lead
our lives.
The sun will shine, the moon will hide.
Be with me always never leave my side.
Behind those pretty eyes,
you wear a mask of loneliness.
Tried to help, this help you didn't need.
Are you to hide forever,
paying the price of loving too quickly
then losing your love to greed?
Reaching for more than one would need.
Leaves me standing as if I was still on my knees.

Bracelet of Charms

When did you receive your first charm?
Did you wear it on a bracelet to keep him upon
your arm?
Gave you, Avery J. in a special way.
First one being a paw print and a miniature rose.
Placed on black leather and a twist of steel.
Nothing like what was shared, yet this made it real.
Kept adding from there so these charms you
can wear.
With hunting boots and short, short hair.
To the moon and back plus a watering can,
given in love, keeping you smitten was the plan…
Swamps in the hills, walks down the lane.
All for this beauty and still can't call Her name.

THE
P.O.W.—M.I.A.
BRACELET
This bracelet honors the man whose name is inscribed and includes the date he was lost. It should be worn with the vow that it will not be removed until the day the Red Cross is allowed into Hanoi and can assure his family of his status and that he receives the humane treatment due all men.
★ ★ ★
Distributed by VIVA (Voices in Vital America) a non-profit, non-political national student
SGT. BOBBY HARRIS
©VIVA—1970

Ring of Lude... Bracelet of Words

It was but a charm,
it won't do any harm.
If anything can be said,
it will forever keep him in your head.

September 17, 1974

Small leather cord, tied with a knot.
Friendship bracelet is all you got.
Black leather and a hook of metal,
to hang the charms given by him.
A bracelet of swivels made in
the Hill Country.
Given in a grace, most I've ever seen.
Take all I've planted and
give it away, cut the flowers,
move the trees, want just what
can't be had.
It was but a charm.
It won't do any harm.

February 26, 2023

Looking for the Big Trees

The first day I saw you — I knew something
lovely was about to come true.
Later I knew tears would be shed,
the skies would cease to be blue.
I loved and cared not knowing
or wanting any but you.
The day has come to pass,
I wonder if you felt this way too.
Cut with a saw, dug with a spade.
Hope I planted more than I slayed…

Snow Angel

So easy it would be to leave…
Once gone nothing remains except for your song.
Words will be written saying where we went wrong.
So easy it would be to leave.
Touched by the wind — while crying in the snow.
My heart you have seen- the soul you will
never know.
Listening to the sea.
Wondering as I walk in the sand.
Not knowing about tomorrow — feel like flying,
not wanting to land.
Talking of being free — laughing as the planet
is crying,
is all there seems to be.
Stop while there is time, or you will surely be rid
of me.

Hear a Tear Fall...
or a Lady's Tresses Orchid

Ever hear a teardrop fall?
Ever see a snowflake break?
Ever see the wind change colors?
Ever care more for yourself,
than you do others?
Float away for your own sake.
No tears have She — doesn't even remember me.
Feel the sea flow and touch the soul.
Return in the future and collect the toll.

Now

She sat as a Queen watching the world before her
Closed Her eyes for nothing around could hold
Her sight.
Within and above She went — to a place her
mother had
showed Her many years before.
Here was found — things only She wished for —
came around.
A pool of sweet - perfumed lotion in which to bathe.
A couch on which to dream, a stream into which
She could gaze, seeing how the heavens were made.
All these visions were nice tho not enough
To keep Her soul from becoming ice.
Here she stayed for lack of space…

Then

Having all that was wished — a longing remained.
For the place to give Her life a much-needed spice.
Inward She stared—none spoke, none dared.
Even as She stopped to listen for a whisper
or for even a shout, none could help.
So, She left in doubt.
never to be without…
Only in her time, be it days or decades.
All who have known her
to those who have tried.
Mostly to the ones whom were trusted
only to have lied.
Touched by the vanity of beauty…
She has no doubt…
doing all in her power
never to be without.

got it al
together
a lot
of ways
you can
smoke
Who are you
GOODBYE TO
THE BLIND
SLASH DEAD
KID'S HOOCH

Forever

He had Her with the flowers and an unsigned collage.
Gifted from Her in the past, impressed by
his remembering
and a wink in caring as he told Her it would be.
Of the few memories that last,
His was a real blast from the past.
He spoke of flowers growing in a valley near
his home.
Within his heart burned the desire to stay.
He took a flower — placed it in her hand —
Saying it would only wilt at Her command.
Seeds from this flower, She planted in the soil
of kindness and mercy — growing into a garden
of love.
Spreading with each season and every word
She spoke.
Flowers to share, petals tossed into the air.
Some laughed at this romantic lady — as thru
the passing seasons She danced.
In her garden, giving flowers to each that touch
her hand.
If this isn't for you, no doubt you carry a burden
of doom.
Open your heart and within this flower will bloom.

1957

Note in a Bottle

All I can give now is the time to take
the note out of the bottle.
Where all these poems have been kept.
Never really wrote about the job as a gardener.
until the end… how cool is this?
During a fantasy haze lasting 46 circles
around the sun…
Thank you for returning to my life…
As I wrote hoping for this to become truth.
Sworn to secrets… bound by more
Never can say enough but always…
thanking time… for it gave us more.

April 5, 2022

THE NORMAN BRYANT
COLONIAL
COUNTRY CLUB
COLONIAL
COUNTRY CLUB
Clay Courts
Temporarily
Closed

Lone Flier

Looked but didn't feel — pasted the time
so, I guess it's real — crossed a stream carrying
a dream.
Returned and there was a flood —
all I carried was a bucket of mud.
Knew from the first — it wouldn't be any better.
Just figured it couldn't get any worse.
Then again it wasn't anything like what I knew first…
Gone to return is doubtful…
What did you learn?
Hot when it's hot… cold when it's cold…
Do something now before you get old.

Save the Last One

Wind of nite — take my fright
Run it along — may you bring another song.
For if not — wind of nite
Bring back my fright.
Known then forgotten — loved then hated
Hunted then saved — for another day.
Who can say — why all
the large animals went away?
Wasn't their choice or for lack of room.
From the Carolina Parakeet, passenger pigeon
and the Ivory-Billed Wood Pecker.
All gone way too soon... When is the
time for extinction?
Some gone before we could see,
thus the saying "can't see the
forest for the trees."
Hoofed whitetail and an occasional bear
along with the wildhog kicking
up mud into the air.
Only high fenced galleries from
the west they come...
Enclosed and or shot is the main
reason large beasts we have not...

Alicia

Sadder eyes have i seen
Closer places have i been
But never as glad will I be…
Until Alicia again — can I talk to thee.
Cathy and Bro Tim — swam so deep
I might have drowned — if not for him.
Flew so high nearly reached the sky
Forever Thames will you flow…
May each new day… teach you
Something ya didn't know.

Purple Rings

Plants will grow… for plants we know
If you want to love… gotta let it show.
Mushrooms are free… in pastures will they be
In every month they can grow…
To show us more of what we need to know.
Purple rings the rains bring…
Now and forever may they grow…
Spores in the air… carried by the breeze
All the knowledge… pretty as you please.

Untitled

Roses of Tyler — dozen for a dollar
Children sell by the hour —
save for the sun
Long for the shade — gotta give Momma
the money you made
Young and old — many stories unknown
Could be you — could be me
Can't tell now — just wait and see
What a pleasure it might be
To sell roses in Tyler — dozen for a dollar.

June 1977

Dallas Malice

Moved but what does it say?
Turn around, do it another day.
Dancer at Geno's — wonder what she knows
Where it comes — maybe where it goes
Not bad money for the day
Talked but never asked to stay
She walked in the door — see you again
See you no more
Don't know you — Don't know me
Passed that day — all the better for me
Breeze through the heat — in June it's 102°
Met people upon the street
Careful to speak — careful to do
Dance so lively — dance so vain
Why you dance — can you explain?

June 1977

Blue Northern

On we walk — on we talk
With a few reminders of the times, we brought.
If it were now — if it were later
Could you tell, it's always hot as hell in Dallas?
Stone walls, concrete streets, toll roads and
trash heaps.
Fish in a bowl, me without a goal.
Probably be able to find one,
if the summers weren't so hot
and the winters weren't so cold.
Feel the wind thru the cinder blocks,
blowing across the plains.
Bringing in a blue northern with either ice or rain.

Withdrawn or Leaving Dallas

Joined but not finished…
Drawn but not colored…
Nailed but not built…
Don't know why I wrote this
Just kinda how I felt.
Sitting under a willow, this is what I drew…
Thirteen pictures and a painting of you.
Not without reason — not without pain…
If I could do it over — this, I would do again
Hard to answer — harder to explain
Why the wind doesn't blow — why it doesn't rain?

MACEL PALMER BROWN

Stoned Words

Engraved in stone are the words you have
left when you're finally gone.
Sad as it seems this is true, wonder what
I'll write when we bury you?
I write for my friends as we all meet the end.
For more pasting I wish not to write.
Do me a favor and live past the night.
Where we can laugh again and dance in the light.
As your friends go — treasure all you can save.
Little drops of ink upon the last page.
All my sad writings these I have saved,
Perhaps only to burn them later
Or bury them too — deep in a cave.

Seeds or Bulbs

Who's going to be listening — when the words
finally come?
If in waiting so long — the grass has dried.
and the water is all gone.
In the beauty of a flower — you can see it's need.
To change amidst the falling rain,
To change in the glowing sun,
Change from a budding flower to the hopeful seed.
Saving seeds is a skill bringing joy.
Having them sprout is all it's about.
Saved through time and still upon the vine
practice this if you will
something precious you see…
Passed from one to another then
back again… Seeds can pay
the bill… If you can learn the skill

Occupy
July 4

Hey You

Saw You before yet never was aware
of the sweetness in that smile and the raven
color of Your long silky hair.
Or the silence in the room — when You're not there.
Never was aware of the song in Your laughter.
Or of the longing in Your stare — for what
You want and how much You care.

Austin, June 1975

Started this rhyme years ago,
sure didn't figure it still had lines to go.
Crossed paths dozens of times,
never to see you but always caring my friend.
From sand bars under the bridge
to your dad and his sage advice
"Don't split out too far"
not sure what he meant,
not sure to this day.
But somehow those words
carry a lot of sway…

Ander

To seek the things wanted — to value the
things learned
Crawling became a walk — a walk became a run
Run for fun — run to get away
Lifting feet high and sprint to the new day.
Marvel at the wonders and all the birds as they fly
Cast the net wide, bide the time given…
For all your treasures lie in your heart hidden.
Good day to be outside…
Toting a bucket, tossing the rocks.
Feeding the chickens, racing the clock
Memphis mess at his best.
Angel gifts of Paw Pals and books
walking down this path with
you has been a treasure
shared by only a few…

Shadows of Flowers

Reasons I ask — reasons I was given
For some reason — these always seem forbidden
But why leave so soon?
Isn't there time — isn't there room?
Shadows on the wall — show a presence near
Yet departure is certain — so is the fear
If not for a year — for at least another beer
Placed between the pages — hoping to last the ages
Are the flowers of time — along with these words
of rhythm

New Dawn

These words are all I have — sent out into the crowd
Written on paper instead of shouting out loud
Toil through the day — looking around and this
was found
While picking blackberries that had fallen to
the ground
Searching for a dream — looking among the privet
For the New Dawn Rose — finding it full of thorns
Yet the fragrance so sweet to the nose...
Here lies the dream — not really what was in mind
But nevertheless — this Rose we did find.
May the New Dawn bring you cheer
May your halls bedecked, with holly, ferns
and laughter with the scent of Sweet Olive in the air.

Rock-Bottle... Broken Glass

Glass thrown into the sea may float or may sink
All is lost if we treat the oceans like a sink
Glass broken and tumbled in the sand
Becomes smooth — handled without a cut
Wasteful and lazy — rich and bored
This can't be our legacy — for the land isn't ours to waste
Yet this is what has been done — cause everything is a race.
Hurry along at this pace — pick up the trash
And put it in its place.

Pot Stirrer

She stares at the candle that sits upon a skull
She had cast a spell once — in vengeance and hate…
She regrets it now — but the brew is done
Forgiveness is too late — only in time can
She correct the mistake… The brew is
always cooking
It simmers and boils — glitter and perfume will
it make
Years later still She stirs this stew…
Sweet and sour it is all for you
She waits and She cooks — beauty is her curse
With a look that chills — all around the fire
The flame is dark without a spark — how can this be?
All this magic and misery cast upon me.

...THE
End